Life Wisdom for Young Adults

LaFoy Orlando Thomas III, Esq.

DEDICATION

I dedicate this book to Dries, my six-year-old son. I love you. You are an amazing gift from the Most High.

CONTENTS

.

ACKNOWLEDGMENTS

I give all thanks and praise to the Most High.
I am aware that without your mercy and favor
I would be nothing and no more.

CHAPTER 1
EXAMINING AUTHOR'S TOP
FINANCIAL PRINCIPLES

#1 "Gold labors diligently and contentedly for the wise owner who finds for it profitable employment, multiplying even as the flocks of the field." – The Richest Man in Babylon

Gold, in this case, represents money that is invested and positioned in an environment where it can grow and gain the benefit of compounding. For young adults, it is important to know that time is on your side as an investor. If you are between the ages of 18-25, you likely have at least 35 years until retirement. If an investor was to make a one-time investment of $5,000.00 in a tax-deferred account, such as a Roth IRA, and allow it to grow for 35 years, the total account can grow to over $260,000 if you can grow your account by an average of 12% per year. If you can grow your account by an average of 14% a year, the total grows to over $490,000, all from a one-time $5,000 investment.

Most brokerage houses, such as TD Ameritrade and Fidelity, allow you to sign up for dividend reinvestment, which allows the firm to purchase more shares, even if only partial shares, on your behalf without charging you a fee when one of your investments distributes a dividend. My largest fund holding, XLK, which is the technology sector exchange-traded fund, currently has a 1.6% yield and I reinvest the dividends when they are paid out every quarter. It needs no action on my behalf to reinvest the dividends other than me signing up for dividend reinvestment. I strongly recommend dividend reinvestment for all investors and it will likely amplify your long-term returns as you can see from the difference between growing your money by 14% versus 12%. That 2% difference resulted in an additional $230,000 over 35 years.

Although I have had plenty of success picking individual public stocks throughout the years, I now prefer, and recommend, buying index funds that cover sectors and not just small industries, such as semiconductors. One industry, such as semiconductors or cyber security, can experience long periods of lagging the market and can cause you to miss out on the gains of a bull market. There is nothing cool about watching the overall stock market go higher and higher and your investments not participate in the rally. The same applies to individual stocks. Although a company can be in great financial condition, a company can remain unpopular with investors for years before it starts to be aggressively accumulated by investors, which is what often causes stock prices to run up.

Another reason that I prefer to buy and hold index funds long term is because I've adopted the concept of gaining wealth by creating versus competing. Buying and selling stocks for a living is not only time consuming but also energy draining and distracts you from your purpose. One of my favorite books on the subject of money is *The Science of Getting Rich* by Wallace D. Wattles. In his book, he preaches the importance of doing things in a certain way and making sure that whatever line of business that you're in that you give more in use value than you receive in cash value. He also preaches to gain your wealth operating in the creative realm instead of on the plane of competition. When acting as an active trader of individual stocks, the goal is to sell before the price declines, which is almost the equivalent of selling a car to someone right before you expect the engine to die.

#2 Although jobs serve an important purpose in our society, they are not a viable long-term solution to the problems faced by those seeking financial independence and generational wealth. A job should be used to develop your work ethic, master your craft, and save money to start your own venture.

In the large majority of cases, children cannot inherit the jobs of their parents or grandparents. Although there are some cases of nepotism, typically when the company believes that your services are no longer desired, the company moves on while breaking any and all attachments. This is one of the reasons why when you are an employee for someone, you have to effectively use them while they are using you. This isn't meant in a negative sense. The services that you provide for a business often create streams of income for that business for years to come. However, if the employee doesn't successfully invest his earnings, when the relationship ends with the employer, the employee no longer benefits from the relationship.

So many people are shocked when they dedicate 20 or more years to a company and are then let go unceremoniously whenever a decision maker from the company feels like it's time to move on. You can never forget that your place of employment is likely a for-profit establishment that prioritizes the bottom line over your need to feed your family. So if you are going to work for someone, please remember to save money to invest and start your own business. That way the money that you invested can continue to work for you and both parties will likely continue to benefit long after the relationship ends.

Also, there is great value in having a business where you can help to develop the work ethic of your children and grandchildren. Employing your descendants is often mutually gratifying because employees often prefer to work for a business that they will likely inherit and are likely to take their work more seriously.

Probably the biggest turn off to working as an employee long term, besides the loss of freedom, is the fact that your earning potential is likely to be limited, even if you generate a billion dollars worth of revenue for your company. In most businesses, however, if you generate a billion dollars worth of revenue, as an entrepreneur, you will likely end the year a very wealthy man or woman. Time is one of the most valuable commodities, if not the most valuable, that we have and it should be used as much as possible to build generational wealth for your family instead of solely for your boss' family.

#3 Forming a limited liability company to either build a business or to act as an investment holding company to protect assets from creditors is sound risk management.

A limited liability company, or LLC, is a pass-through tax entity that provides limited liability to its owners and operators. Many people think that an LLC or corporation provides complete liability protection against its owners and operators, but that is definitely not the case. A person, regardless of entity choice, is always personally responsible for his or her own torts, such as negligence and fraud. Also, the business may be held responsible as well under the legal doctrine of respondeat-superior.

Structuring the proper business entity with your secretary of state, such as an LLC or corporation, protects the owner personally against contracts, debts of the business, and, depending on the situation and jurisdiction, the actions of employees. If a CEO commits an act of negligence that violates the business judgment rule, he or she can be held personally liable. Owners and operators of an LLC, however, can obtain directors and officers insurance to help protect against many unintentional torts.

The business judgment rule creates a presumption that the officers acted in good faith and took reasonable action to be informed. However, if a shareholder is able to demonstrate that an officer acted without regard for the best interest of the business or failed to become informed regarding a material decision, the officer is likely to be held personally responsible and in need of protection from his directors and officers insurance.

Being a pass-through tax entity, the profits and losses of the LLC pass down to the owners and the owners claim the profit or loss on their individual tax returns. This is different from a corporation since a corporation's operators must file a separate tax return for the business. Having an LLC allows entrepreneurs to deduct business losses from personal income, which often offsets tax liability to some degree. Losses from a corporation, unless one files for an S-corporation, cannot be deducted from personal income to offset tax liability. This is important because many businesses, even the ones that are eventually successful, lose money in the early years.

Also, forming an LLC to act as an investment holding company is a great way to protect your assets from personal creditors. If all of your assets are owned personally by you, a creditor can recover any judgment from your personal assets, often times before the asset has had a chance to multiply in value. However, if a creditor was to obtain a judgment against a person, the creditor would not be able to reach the assets held by the debtor's LLC. At best, the creditor would be able to obtain a charging order, which attaches the judgment to the assets or distributions that are due to the debtor.

For example, if the LLC pays distributions quarterly or annually to its members (LLC's name for its owners), the debtor's portion can be recovered by the creditor who has a charging order. However, the creditor cannot satisfy the debt by taking money from the LLC's bank account or by taking other assets from the business. The laws regarding charging orders varies by state, but the creditor also cannot replace the debtor by obtaining his or her ownership interest in the LLC, which allows the management team to continue conducting business with its intended management team. Some states, however, allow for a debtor's membership interest in an LLC to be foreclosed upon to satisfy a judgment. Forming an LLC gives the founders the assurance that the creditors and ex-spouses of the members won't be showing up to vote or help manage the business.

The LLC is my preferred business entity as long as there are no immediate plans to go public, in which case I'd likely form a traditional corporation. Also, if I knew that my business would be seeking venture capital to grow, I'd likely form a corporation in that instance as well. Most venture capitalists will only invest in a traditional corporation.

#4 A Roth IRA should be used for those with employment income to ensure tax-free income in retirement. Assets in a Roth IRA grow tax deferred are can be withdrawn during retirement tax free.

A Roth IRA is an easy-to-open investment account that allows an investor to invest up to

$6,000, of after-tax money, annually into a tax-deferred account. The money in a Roth IRA grows tax deferred and withdrawals taken after age 59 ½ are completely tax free.

Also, money contributed (the money that you put in the account) to a Roth IRA can be withdrawn (taken back out of the account) at any time, at any age, without any penalty or tax. The Roth IRA is a great vehicle to build generational wealth and can be opened with just about any broker online, including TDAmeritrade, Fidelity, and E*TRADE.

Some people prefer the traditional IRA over the Roth IRA because of the traditional IRA's immediate tax benefits. With a traditional IRA, the money invested works as a tax deduction and reduces the corresponding year's tax liability. However, in retirement the investor is required to pay tax on withdrawals at the person's tax rate for that year. With a Roth IRA, contributions are not tax deductible but all of the profits during retirement are completely tax free.

I think it is more advantageous to pay taxes now on your $6,000 per year contribution and then in retirement have the opportunity to withdraw your millions without any tax liability. I'd much rather pay taxes on thousands than pay taxes on millions. It is important to also note that both the traditional IRA and the Roth IRA grow tax deferred, which means that capital gains and dividends in both accounts create no tax liability as long as the money remains in the account. The differences are the tax treatment of contributions and, in retirement, the tax treatment of withdrawals. The traditional IRA creates a tax break now but no tax break in retirement. The Roth IRA creates no tax break now but creates an abundance of tax free income in retirement.

Another benefit of both a traditional IRA and the Roth IRA is that most states protect IRA's from creditor's claims, which makes IRAs great vehicles for building generational wealth. Protection from creditors and the ability to grow tax deferred are tremendous benefits, and the Roth has the added advantage, like I said, of creating a tax-free fortune in retirement.

#5 Equity crowdfunding opportunities, such as those listed on Wefunder.com, should be considered when allocating investment assets. Although large, multi-national companies typically have the smallest chance of failure, startups with proven product-market fit and fast growing sales create better opportunities for generating astronomical ROI (return on investment).

Due to a new law called Regulation Crowdfunding, since May of 2016, non-accredited investors can now invest in startups and other stage private companies that were previously only available to the affluent, known as accredited investors.

Many of the greatest investment returns are achieved by early-stage investors in companies that grow and either get acquired or go public. Not all startup companies make great investments, and I recommend performing due diligence before making any investment, public or private. Although I've invested in a couple of companies prior to them reaching seven-figure annual revenue, I prefer private companies with over $1,000,000 in annual revenue and revenue growth of at least 40% annually.

Investing in companies with large and growing revenues substantially reduces the risk that is inherent when investing in early-stage companies. The reason is that the company has likely established what is known as product-market fit. This means that there is a strong market for what the business has to offer. Also, a company with over $1,000,000 in revenue is more likely to be able to attract a venture capital firm or another investor before the company runs out of capital. A company with very little or no revenue is usually at least several years away from becoming attractive to venture capitalists, which means possibly even longer than 10 years before an exit event.

Most companies that are raising money on platforms such as Wefunder have yet to seek venture capital in the form of a Series A round but are also further along than the typical seed-stage investment. Once a company is able to raise a venture capital round, revenue and profit growth rates are likely to grow tremendously due to the new funding and business support. Being able to recognize and invest in a company that is growing fast in an attractive industry, prior to the venture capitalists, creates the opportunity to grow $1,000 to over $200,000 or more in 10 years or less in a best-case scenario. Imagine investing in Facebook or Google prior to the earliest of venture capitalists. In the case of huge success stories, such as Facebook and Google, a $1,000 early-stage investment would have likely made you a millionaire at least several times over.

It is important to keep in mind, however, that many early-stage companies fail and the potential to lose your entire investment is relatively high. In addition to thinking logically and performing due diligence before making every investment, it is important to diversify your holdings and to not put all of your money in one or two companies. If you have $5,000 available to allocate to private investments, I recommend dividing the money between 10-20 companies. An amount as small as $100, which is the minimum investment for many companies on Wefunder, invested in the right company can deliver an astronomical return.

In addition to having a higher chance of failing compared to the large, multinational companies, there are also limited means of liquidating your investments prior to the company being acquired or going public, which means you likely won't be able to sell your investment prior to an exit event. This makes investments in private companies defacto long-term investments, and an investor should only invest money into private companies that the investor is confident that he or she will not need before the hoped-for exit event.

#6 Privately owned businesses, stocks, real estate, and intellectual property that can by monetized, such as books or music publishing, are the foundations of

generational wealth.

A key characteristic of generational wealth is the ability of the owned assets to provide substantial income for future generations. If a basketball player, for example, makes $50,000,000 during his playing career and fails to live beneath his means and doesn't invest his money wisely, there will likely be very little for future generations to inherit.

Many people think that they have achieved financial security after earning a certain amount of money, but without financial literacy the money isn't secure and remains at risk to being depleted due to poor spending habits or unscrupulous advisors.

Having a diversified asset base is of the utmost importance, in my opinion, and should grow to include private companies, public stocks, real estate, and intellectual property. Private companies can either be businesses that you start and own or businesses that you invest in on platforms such as Wefunder. Public stocks can include individual stocks, but I recommend broad funds for the average investor to make sure you are always participating during bull markets.

Real estate, when purchased wisely, also has

the potential to provide passive income for generations to come. One of the many advantages of owning real estate, which is real property, is the fact that they are not making any new land, which makes it a finite resource. This automatically has a positive impact on supply and demand factors. As the number of people living on Earth increases, the amount of land in existence, without considering the impact of volcanos or other natural disasters, is basically fixed. Owning land also creates the opportunity to grow your own food, which has increased in importance as food supplies become less trustworthy. Also, the right real estate investment will be in a strong rental market and have a financial structure where tenant rents are used to pay off the monthly mortgage payments.

It typically takes money to buy the assets mentioned above, but the great thing about intellectual property is that you can create it out of thin air. With a little work, you can transform a thought, or a collection of thoughts, into a generational asset. You can write books, songs, movies, or patent ideas for licensing. Some people spend their entire lives buying assets and others spend their entire lives creating assets that establish wealth for multiple generations. I strongly recommend a combination of both.

#7 It is important to track expenses, create a budget, and intentionally live beneath one's own means. Discretionary income should be used to invest in assets, such as stocks and real estate. However, for the man or woman aware of his or her purpose, the best investment is in your purpose.

The process of tracking your expenses at the end of the month might reveal to you that you spend an unacceptable amount of money on things that are not a priority to you. Having this awareness, you can take action to eliminate unnecessary expenses and allocate more capital to the things that mean the most to you. I heard once from a colleague when I was a financial advisor that "the reason most people don't achieve their goals is because they give up what they want the most for what they want for the moment." Take care to not unintentionally sacrifice your goals by acting on impulse or failing to identify your spending habits by not tracking your expenses.

After tracking your expenses for a couple of months, it is important to decide which expenses deserve a place on the final budget, always keeping your most important financial goals in mind. It is important to always treat yourself to great food and fun times, but consideration should always be given to whatever it is for you that holds the most importance.

When writing your budget, it is important to start with your necessary expenses, such as your rent, utilities, food, transportation, and debt payments. After the necessary expenses, decide how you want to divide the remainder between your savings, investments, and entertainment, which includes traveling and eating at restaurants. After your necessary expenses, you may have $500 a month remaining, for example, that you can choose to allocate as follows: $250 for investments in your Roth IRA, $125 for your vacation fund, and the remaining $125 for monthly entertainment.

Once you are aware of your purpose, I recommend allocating both time and some of your investment money to creating and executing your vision by doing business or sharing your gift with the world in a way that adds value to as many people as possible without taking advantage of anyone. In addition to expenses related to getting your business off the ground, your purpose may require you to spend time and money developing certain innate gifts to prepare them for commercial usage.

#8 Building and managing your credit profile creates the opportunity to use OPM (other people's money) and build wealth at an accelerated pace.

Before applying for your first credit card, I think it is important to first demonstrate to yourself that you have the discipline required to use credit wisely. If you know that you struggle with making wise decisions, I recommend holding off on applying for credit cards because it is very easy to impulsively max out a credit card.

However, after you believe that you have demonstrated a reasonable amount of discipline, applying for your first credit card will put you on the path to building a healthy credit profile. In many cases, since you may not have any credit, you may have to apply for a secured credit card with a company like Capital One, which will require you to make a deposit with the institution in the amount of the desired credit line. The account is secured by your deposit, making it a secured credit card.

In addition to obtaining loans with very low interest rates on items such as cars and home appliances, building a solid credit profile will increase your chances of obtaining business credit and real estate loans at very reasonable rates. Using credit to finance your new business plans and real estate ventures is an example of using other people's money to build generational wealth. Also, credit obtained at low interest rates substantially reduces monthly payments and leaves more capital available for the accumulation of assets and an enjoyable lifestyle.

#9 Term life insurance from reputable organizations should be considered to reduce the chance of economic catastrophe in the event of loss of life to key earners or contributors.

To avoid putting your family members in a potentially compromising situation financially, I recommend that everyone maintain a term life insurance policy. Many companies provide 30-year policy coverage of over $100,000 for less than $20 a month.

There's a significant difference between the cost of whole life insurance, which covers you until you die or stop making payments, and the cost of term life insurance, which covers you for the length of the policy. The savings between the two should be invested in a Roth

IRA or into a business that you use to add value to the world and utilize your gifts.

#10 The best companies and real estate in the world can make bad investments if purchased at horrible valuations. Valuation is key, especially when expecting prolonged holding periods. Buying quality assets, such as stocks and real estate, during recessions and bear markets improves long-term returns exponentially. Although buying assets during economic expansions can be prudent as well, the valuations are usually not nearly as reasonable as when people are panicking during temporary downturns.

The valuation of a business is similar to the appraised value of real property. Although in many cases investors do not buy an entire business, the valuation, or market cap, is what the market participants are saying is the current value of the entire business. In order to buy 1% of a business, you will typically have to pay 1% of its valuation, with the exception of special cases.

It is important to perform your due diligence before making any investment and to make sure that you are able to logically justify the valuation of the business, intellectual asset, or real property before acquisition. If a business has $10,000,000 in revenue, $1,000,000 in net income, and is consistently growing revenue and profits by 5% per year, it would be less than prudent to invest in this business if the valuation was $100,000,000 for example. However, if the valuation was $20,000,000, it may be a reasonable investment if the acquirer has reason to believe it can substantially grow revenue and profits.

The best valuations are usually found during recessions and the beginning of economic recoveries. Although the overall U.S. stock market always recovers after a bear market, which is a drop of 20% or more, many investors panic and sell at depressed valuations and then repurchase after the market has recovered. An investor following such a sequence has greatly disadvantaged his or her long-term returns and would have been better off holding for the long term.

Not always, but the worst valuations are usually found during extended economic expansions that are accompanied by prolonged bull markets, which is the term for consistently rising asset prices. Many times during expansions, investors are willing to pay higher and higher valuations for investments with the expectation that the particular assets will continue to increase in value. All assets eventually peak, even if only for a period, and sometimes it takes decades to break even on assets that were purchased at inflated valuations near the peak in the economic or market cycle.

#11 Reading my book, Generational Wealth: Beginner's Business & Investing Guide, will teach you the basic and in-depth knowledge required to build wealth as an entrepreneur, real estate investor, and as an investor in stocks.

In the third edition of my book *Generational Wealth: Beginner's Business & Investing Guide*, I recommend always keeping dry gun powder for recessions and to buy as many quality assets, at reduced prices, as possible. Buying great investments that are almost certain to recover when the market recovers, such as broad funds and rental properties in healthy markets, helps investors achieve above average long-term returns.

The book also does a great job of teaching readers the fundamentals of economics, stock market investing, real estate investing, starting a business, acquiring a business, and is also a useable guide for understanding contract law. The book is a must read and is available at Amazon.com. Autographed copies of the author's books are available at GWSigned.com.

CHAPTER 2
EXAMINING AUTHOR'S CORE
SPIRITUAL BELIEFS

#1 "Knowledge is consciousness of reality. Reality is the sum of the laws that govern nature and of the causes from which they flow." – Ancient Egyptian Proverb

Many people in the world are out of touch with reality and are walking through life unconsciously, not aware of the power of their thoughts, intentions, and deeds. One of the main culprits for the world being so deceived is the programming, by way of television, to the human mind.

For spiritual consciousness and the ability to observe and confirm universal law, I recommend walking in parks with your bare feet in the grass. I also recommend meditating, practicing yoga, and ceasing the consumption of animal products and fluoride-filled tap water. Animal products are unhealthy and create horrible karma since innocent animals are separated from their families and often murdered without any consideration or sympathy. Fluoride causes the calcification of your pineal gland, also known as the third eye. Fluoride also causes the body to store aluminum, which is a common denominator of Alzheimer patients. I recommend drinking spring water only.

Sun gazing, or holding eye contact with sun, is another great practice that will help you activate your pineal gland and boost your mood. The sun provides the body with natural vitamin D. It is also important to monitor your thoughts and to pay attention when the universe responds to your energy. Without paying attention to the universe's responses to your thoughts, intentions, or deeds, one is likely to repeat certain lessons, or hard times, over and over until satisfactory advancement and completion.

#2 "Man must learn to increase his sense of responsibility and of the fact that everything he does will have its consequences." – Ancient Egyptian

Proverb

Many people believe that an act, criminal or otherwise, can be done without a witness. I would like to remind you that there is always a witness to all of your thoughts and all of your deeds. After going unconscious, a person often loses awareness of the karmic effects of his or her behavior and may even justify unimaginable deeds.

Very often, people who are unjust with others become enraged with they are treated unfairly. It is very important to always try your best to live righteously and to put your best foot forward when attempting to accomplish any worthy goal. The universe bears witness to all of your deeds and rewards the diligent. My advice is to try your best to think good thoughts, speak good words, and to do good deeds. It is also important to recognize when you're wrong, seek to correct the mistake or behavior, and then forgive yourself and others who you believe have wronged you.

#3 "The half-wise, recognizing the comparative unreality of the universe, imagine that they may defy its laws—such are vain and presumptuous fools, and they are broken against the rocks and torn asunder by the elements by reason of their folly. The truly wise,

knowing the nature of the universe, use law against laws; the higher against the lower; and by the art of alchemy transmute that which is undesirable into that which is worthy and thus triumph. Mastery consists not in abnormal dreams, visions and fantastic imaginings or living, but in using the higher forces against the lower-escaping the pains of the lower planes by vibrating on the higher. Transmutation, not presumptuous denial, is the weapon of the master." —
The Kybalion

When you are engaged in negative thinking, for example, and then you hit your foot on a hard object, please do not consider it a coincidence. Everything happens according to law. When you engage in questionable behavior that results in disharmony, please take note of your communication from the universe. Don't be a fool and think that you may behave in any manner and still maintain a peaceful, harmonious life. Wake-up calls often become more intense if prior wake-up calls have been disregarded. The misuse of free will has always had its consequences.

When experiencing disharmony, it is important to adjust your alchemy formula by switching the frequency of your thoughts, which changes the frequency of your feelings. In addition, you must set all good intentions and modify any intentions that are out of alignment with your highest self. Returning to harmony is often as simple as cleaning your heart of any malice or ill will, setting positive intentions, forgiving yourself and others, and making a genuine commitment to live as righteously as possible.

Many people, however, suffer from presumptuous denial, which causes them to ignore the messages sent from the universe in response to the person's thoughts, intentions, or deeds. If every time you do a certain thing it results in a disharmonious situation, please do not disregard your message from the universe. The message is intended to steer you in the right direction. Many of us have learned right from wrong from television, music, and other external forces that are not in alignment with universal law.

A special note from my study of numerology: people born on the 16th of any month often need traumatic wake-up calls in order to return to consciousness. Less intense wake-up calls are often disregarded as "life," and life lessons are often not learned when one fails to connect cause and effect. If you were born on the 16th of any month, please take great care to acknowledge your wake-up calls when they are still gentle and not force the universe to constantly increase the intensity of your wake-up calls.

In numerology, 16 is a karmic number which represents an abuse of love. It's often associated with adultery or taking advantage of the love of others. After learning about the karmic number 16, I wanted to know why people born on the 16th often need traumatic wake-up calls. The answer that came to me was that since love is a representation of the Most High, to abuse love can be compared to waging war against the Most High, and the measure of the transgression is likely equal to the measure of unconsciousness that the person encounters. To abuse love is a very serious transgression and intentionally abusing the love of another should be avoided at all costs, and this applies to everyone, not just people born on the 16th.

#4 "Every Cause has its Effect. Every Effect has its Cause. Everything happens according to Law. Chance is but a name for Law not recognized. There are many planes of causation, but nothing escapes the Law." – The Kybalion

Very similar to #2 above, please keep in mind that every cause has its effect and every effect has its cause. Everything happens according to law, many of which we can observe and confirm. When tempted to act in a way that is likely going to cause unnecessary disharmony in another, please think of the potential consequences, pass the test, and evolve to the next level.

Taking care to only put energy into the universe that you are okay with returning to you will help you to carry yourself in such a way that is likely to support your creation of the life that you desire. However, if one is to believe that there is no correlation between cause and effect, he or she is likely to have a very hard time creating the life desired, and the person is likely to think that both good and bad luck are just random responses from the universe.

#5 "When there is no enemy within, the enemies outside cannot hurt you." – African Proverb

I consider the enemy within the entity that we refer to as our ego, which I compare to the concept of Satan, the devil. Pride, being an extension of the ego, has similar desires as the ego: to destroy its host and others. Other enemies, or negative spirits, that I believe grow from the ego, include hate, jealousy, envy, selfishness, extreme anger, revenge, irresponsibility, excessive lust, and carelessness. Take care to note that this is not an exhaustive list.

Spirits that wish to place us outside of divine alignment enter us in many ways, including from listening to negative music that poisons both our conscious and subconscious minds, television, social media, and, most importantly, by disregarding our spirits, or internal compass, that the Most High has given us for both protection and direction. Disregarding the voice of your spirit often, if not always, leads to some level of spiritual unconsciousness that typically requires a new awakening, which often comes by way of a wake-up call. Wake-up calls hurt and often lead to depression, financial trouble, and compromised health.

Protecting our temples from unfriendly energies, or spirits, is very important since we are all responsible for our actions, even when we are unconscious and are blindly creating. If you know, for example, that every time you listen to certain types of rap music that you want to deceive others or perform random acts of violence, voluntarily listening to such music is the equivalent to actually committing the acts. Attempting to justify your behavior with a claim that you were unconscious is silly since you were aware of the effect of such energy on you prior to subjecting yourself to the unaligned energy forces.

#6 "Happiness does not depend on what you have or who you are. It solely relies on what you think." –
Buddha

The mind is a very powerful tool that can be used to create any emotion imaginable. Considering that the choice is ours to choose our emotional state, it makes sense to choose to be happy and to concentrate on thoughts that are likely to manifest into our desired reality. One of the most powerful methods of maintaining a state of bliss is to remain in a state of gratitude: gratitude for your life, home, food, clothes, savings, investments, family, and whatever else comes to mind for which you have genuine appreciation.

Focusing on the positive things in life appears to act as a magnet and attract more things that cause genuine happiness and displays of gratitude. However, if a man, for example, focuses on all of the things that cause him to be sad, he is likely to experience sadness.

Many people struggle and feel powerless when it comes to controlling the thoughts of the mind, and meditation is a great method to strengthen the muscle that is required to control your own thoughts. When a person is unable to control his or her own thoughts, the person is likely to be either controlled or irritated by them. Sometimes the irritation of one's thoughts is strong enough to cause depression. To meditate, find a quiet place to sit and cross your legs. It's important to find a place where you can relax and feel comfortable. Then, for at least five minutes, observe your breathing as much as possible without consciously controlling inhales or exhales. When thoughts come to mind, without judging them, just return to listening to your breathing for as long as possible.

The more that you practice meditating, the easier it will be to remain still and the stronger your mind's power will be with regard to controlling your own thoughts. The power to control and eliminate unwanted thoughts is required to maintain harmony within, reach peak performance, and realize your full potential in any area of life.

Because karma often returns on the mental plane only, this is another reason why it is so important to try your best to protect your karma since an unstable mind is usually unable to focus or accomplish nearly as much as a person who is in possession of a healthy mind.

#7 The universe has a law that I describe as the law of balance. Living balanced is not an option, but a law, and violating the law is a transgression. Getting rich by perpetually neglecting your family, health, or spiritual responsibilities, for example, is a transgression similar to a person getting rich by robbing a bank.

It is very important to prioritize living a balanced lifestyle. It is our duty to nourish ourselves physically, mentally, spiritually, and emotionally. We all have a duty to add value to the world in our own unique way. We also have a duty to spend time with and add value to our families and communities. A person working 100 hours per week often doesn't make time for many of the duties that we all have as humans.

For example, taking care of the body by exercising and consuming whole foods is often neglected by people on a particular mission. Proper cleaning of the home and body is also often neglected. And, needless to say, time with family members is often taken for granted as well when a person is on the unbalanced path. Many people proudly proclaim to have tunnel vision, which often means that only one thing matters to the person and it is often related to either acquiring financial resources or a companion. Obviously, a one-track mind results in an unbalanced lifestyle, which is a transgression. Like other transgressions, a person often goes spiritually unconscious after traveling the path of a particular purpose without balance.

Like any other universal law, when the law is violated, wake-up calls are received and, if disregarded, often result in compromised health, financial trouble, and family instability. Balance is not a choice but a law that the wise are aware of and honor with great respect.

If a young person, for example, believes that he can spend the ages of 18-25 playing video games while striving for nothing else, he may experience wake-up calls in the form of becoming homeless, having disharmony within his family, or by meeting people who can add great value to his life but who are turned off by the idea of him spending so much time playing video games. The universe sends wake-up calls in many different forms, so please stay mindful of your responses from the universe.

On the flipside, if a person during the ages of 18-25 believes that he can spend all of his waking hours building his business or working overtime at his job, he may experience wake-up calls in the form of a loss of important social connections, missing of important events, family disharmony, and chronic illnesses. Also, the business or job may become compromised as well despite the fact that the business or job has been receiving an undivided portion of the person's time and energy.

The goal should always be to establish and maintain internal harmony, and a person can only have internal harmony when there is harmony with the surrounding external forces. When a person is unbalanced, the universe often allows external forces to release vibrations that lead to a lack of internal harmony. Sometimes, however, the disharmony starts internally, such as with a health scare or a disturbed mind.

#8 Although the Most High is the ultimate creator, we must acknowledge that we are all alchemists and have the power and responsibility to co-create our own realities, and harmony is determined by the sum of our thoughts, intentions, and deeds.

With words such as fate and destiny being planted into the minds of our youth without proper understanding, it is no surprise that many people walk throughout life without purpose and with the belief that everything that will ever happen to them has already been decided. A lot of people are hopeless because they have been convinced that no matter what they do, things will not work out for them. People with this mind frame often use their parents or other family members as examples of people who worked hard and honestly but still failed to create the life desired.

One of the problems with comparing yourself to others is the fact that no one, except for the Most High, has all of the relevant factors that acted as variables to create the resulting reality. A person, for example, may work hard for 60 years but fail to create substantial value for others and, therefore, end up working for minimum wage and never establishing wealth. To create wealth, it is a good idea to develop any talent that you have that can add value to a large number of people and then work to bring awareness to the product or service that you are offering. Staying persistent and honoring universal law are both of the utmost importance while on your journey.

Although we may be destined to learn certain lessons during this lifetime, the choice appears to be mostly ours with regard to how the lessons will be learned. There are both easy and hard ways to learn our required lessons, and this is one of the reasons why honoring your wake-up calls, while the intensity is still mild, is so important.

Once a person slows down, goes within, and reflects consistently, he realizes that he is a god with the power and responsibility to create dutifully. However, it is important to remain humble and always acknowledge that your power comes from a higher power and, therefore, one should never compare himself to the Most High. You are a co-creator and the power is yours to use universal law to create either the life desired or a life full of consequences that cause constant disharmony.

#9 Meditation is essential to optimal physical, mental, and spiritual health. Meditation strengthens the mind's ability to focus and also helps re-align one with one's true self and divine purpose.

In addition to strengthening the muscle that is required to control your thoughts, meditation also helps a person return to his or her true self by removing portions of the domestication for which much of society has been subjected. When the mind is allowed to run wild, it is hard for a person to go within and follow his spirit because the voices of the mind are too loud. When the mind is quiet and controlled by its host, the person can begin to hear and interpret the messages from the universe. However, a person with a loud and uncontrolled mind is comparable to a computer having a debilitating and destructive virus.

If you are having trouble controlling your thoughts it is imperative to start meditating immediately, preferably multiple times per day. Meditation has also been known to lower blood pressure, reduce stress, and assist the body in its self-healing process. Also, until a person has control over his or her own mind, it is important to try even harder to avoid energy forces that are not in alignment with universal law and your divine purpose. Television and radio programming are tools that literally program the hearts and minds of men, so take heed. Like it or not, a part of you is being programmed every time you turn on the television or the radio. Be sure to program your heart and mind with software that is likely to help you manifest happiness, wealth, and alignment.

#10 I have observed in the universe what I describe

as the law of karma and mercy, and I believe that karma and mercy are not mutually exclusive. I believe that a person can experience mercy while simultaneously being awakened disharmoniously by a karmic event. Considering that mercy should never be taken for granted, consciously taking care of your karma is prudent and is a form of self-respect and self-love.

For some people, karma is seen as unfair punishment for past deeds. What many people fail to realize is that our actions, in many cases, have actually accumulated much more disharmony than we are actually experiencing ourselves, which is an example of our merciful, loving creator. Many times we are given wake-up call after wake-up call and the universe continues to try to lead us in the right direction.

From observation, I have been able to confirm that when we unconsciously put less-than-desirable energy into the universe, it usually comes back around just strong enough to get our attention. However, when we purposely and consciously put energy into the universe that we know is likely to cause great disharmony, the energy often returns with a vengeance. I believe that it returns in such a manner to deter us from repeating similar behavior or, even more important, from believing that our actions are acceptable and in alignment with universal law.

I've learned that karma and mercy are often working together to help us evolve into the person required to carry out our divine purpose. If it is your intention to truly evolve, then I believe that it is wise to perceive your karma, and the suffering that comes with it, as a great teacher. However, if you've decided to do whatever you want, regardless of how it affects others, I can understand why you would look at karma as if it's an annoying bitch. It's all in perception and intention.

Although we have all been subjected to a great deal of mercy, it is important to not take it for granted or, even worse, as an excuse to misuse our free will. The universe had been designed to get your attention and, if you refuse to honor it, disharmony and great suffering shall surely emerge. Once you are aware of your power and responsibility as an alchemist and co-creator, you also realize that taking care of your karma is a form of self-love. Failing to take good care of your karma is self-abuse and also results in delays with regard to evolving into the best version of yourself.

#11 The day that we, as humans, make peace with both animals and nature will be the day that we make peace with each other; therefore, veganism is a major key to achieving world peace.

Imagine being convicted of no crime whatsoever and waking up locked inside of a cage or in a dirty room or building surrounded by feces, deadly bacteria, and other distressed humans. In the background every day, you hear horrifying screams and what sounds like a universal call for mercy. After living a life without freedom and in an unnatural environment, you are then placed in line in order to be killed so that your body parts may be chopped up and distributed for food, clothing, and byproducts.

Considering how a majority of the world has been conditioned to view animals, how can we expect to have world peace that doesn't include freedom and justice for animals? Based on my knowledge of universal law, I believe it is impossible and actually quite foolish.

An honest observation of the treatment of animals should shock the conscience of any man or woman who hasn't committed themselves to living a life that is dedicated to causing extreme disharmony. In addition to treating animals in a manner that none of us would like reciprocated to us, we are also harming ourselves by consuming animals products, which cause heart disease, diabetes, cancer, stroke, and many chronic illnesses. Please know that this is not an exhaustive list. Most health conditions, including chronic illnesses, can be reversed, however, with a plant-based diet, herbs, meditation, sun light, exercise, and an attitude of gratitude. Dr. Sebi, rest in peace, is a great resource to learn how to eat and heal yourself.

Once a person is able to respect the life of an animal, he or she is much more capable of honoring the life of other humans. If a person has decided not to hurt innocent animals, the same person is likely to not want to hurt innocent humans either. It then evolves into a respect for all living things and you soon realize that you don't even want to pick leaves from trees as it is likely to cause unnecessary harm to a living entity that is actually giving great value to the world.

The key for achieving world peace is the collective returning to our spirits, which is our internal compass from our creator that leads us down the path of righteousness. Once we go within and return to our spirit, we must acknowledge the voice of our spirit when it instructs us to no longer partake in such cruel treatment of any living being. It's important to be true to your spirit and not your mind though. The mind has been thoroughly conditioned by outside forces, and logic and critical thinking can only be counted on to a certain degree when deciding what's righteous or unrighteous. When in doubt, ask your highest self what is right, go within, and you'll quickly find your answer. Be mindful, though, that the mind will want to add its two cents and the heart also, at times, will have something to say. But as I stated in *The Ultimate Book of Wisdom*, be true to thy spirit, not thy heart nor thy mind.

I am convinced that once we make peace with animals, and accept their divinity as well as our own, we will then evolve and elevate to a higher state of consciousness where world peace becomes possible. However, in our current state as a people, our vibrations are too low to achieve world peace because, directly or indirectly, we are participating in the unnecessary suffering and murdering of innocent animals all over the world and are also committing many other hellacious transgressions.

#12 "The kingdom of heaven is within you; and

whoever shall know himself shall find it." – *Egyptian Proverb*

There is no way to know for sure what happens after our physical bodies die, and it is of the utmost importance to seek heaven while you are here on Earth. Many people have accepted the idea of suffering here on Earth and waiting for better days after death. Although it is wise to live your life as if you are preparing to meet the Most High after death, it is important to manifest a life and state of inner harmony that can be compared to heaven.

Once a person is aware of his or her power as a god or goddess, he or she then has the power to create the life desired. The process of finding heaven involves becoming aware of your power and then utilizing it to the best of your ability.

Aligning with your true self and carrying out your purpose also has the ability to promote feelings of euphoria and create a state of bliss that one can compare to the idea of heaven. Studying the metaphysical sciences, such as numerology and astrology, can also make you aware of many of your most powerful natural attributes and the gifts that you were given to fulfil your life's work.

It is very powerful to learn your strengths, weaknesses, opportunities, and threats as an individual. This knowledge of self can act as confirmation to what you already believed were your natural strengths and provide additional confidence while on your path. In one of my books, *The Ultimate Book of Wisdom*, I have a chapter dedicated to the study of numerology, and the book is a great place to start to help you identify your purpose and align with the flow of the universe. For starters, you can enter your date of birth in Google next to the words *life path number* and you will be pleasantly surprised as you learn new things about yourself and also confirm gifts of which you were already partially aware.

#13 Reading my book, The Ultimate Book of Wisdom: A Guide to Spiritual and Financial Prosperity, will give you awareness of your power and responsibility as an alchemist and co-creator of your reality. The book is enlightening, inspirational, and divinely guided.

For more help creating the life that you desire, please read my book, *The Ultimate Book of Wisdom: A Guide to Spiritual and Financial Prosperity*. The book will take you on a life-changing journey that I describe as the road to consciousness and the spirit within. The book is a definite must read and is available on Amazon.com.

CHAPTER 3
PRACTICAL LIFE TIPS

#1 Practicing and mastering the art and science of basic mental math is a great way to improve your capacity to think logically and with foresight. The process of mentally calculating math problems is similar to the process of making sound decisions.

One practice that many children and adults take for granted, likely due to the convenience of calculators, is the process of performing mental math as often as possible. Life provides many chances to use this skill and I believe that it is wise to take advantage and exercise the mental muscles that are required each time the opportunity presents itself.

Many people have trouble thinking logically and I believe one of the reasons is a lack of mental exercises that require people to consider every variable and then follow a step-by-step process without losing sight of the big picture. When performing a math problem mentally, a person has to visualize the numbers, make sure nothing is left out, and then follow a particular method to get an end result. After arriving at an end result, you then have to double check to make sure everything was done correctly.

In order to make logical decisions, a similar process must be followed. A person must visualize the big picture while making sure no variable is missing. All material factors, and many minor, must be considered and then a step-by-step process must be followed in order to make a logical decision. After coming to a decision, or during the process, a person must quickly review each variable to make sure each were given proper consideration and that everything makes sense. Similar to how meditation strengthens the mental muscles required to control your thoughts, working through mental problems, including math, is a great way to develop the skillset that is required to think logically.

#2 A college education can be a great way to develop social skills, start life-long friendships, and acquire the skills required to gain entry into a

particular field. However, college is not the place to go to figure out your purpose.

Many adults are saddled with student loan debt from time spent in college earning degrees that will never be applied professionally. I think it is very unfortunate that society has placed an expectation and a defacto responsibility on each member of our youth to have his or her purpose figured out by the time that he or she graduates from high school. It doesn't make much sense that a person 18 years old is considered responsible enough to collect $250,000 worth of student loan debt but is then considered too young to purchase alcohol. I'm not advocating for the youth to have the right to consume alcohol at an earlier age, but I am pointing out the conundrum related to allowing kids, without awareness of purpose, to indebt themselves for life before they are even considered old enough to drink responsibly.

If you are not sure of your purpose, or chief aim professionally, I recommend spending time after high school self-studying, gaining work experience as an employee or entrepreneur, and traveling. If possible, a combination of the three should be implemented with a balance that nurtures you mentally, physically, spiritually, and emotionally.

However, if you believe that you are aware of your purpose, or if money is no concern, and you value the experience and opportunity to develop socially that college will likely provide, then by all means do not hesitate to enroll. This note is just a warning for people who expect to find themselves while in school. These people often change their majors several times before either graduating or dropping out with a ton of student loan debt, which currently cannot be dismissed in bankruptcy. This situation is only made worse by the fact that, as I alluded to earlier, many of these people will never have a chance to apply themselves professionally in the fields of their studies.

#3 Take great consideration of the partner that you choose for reproduction. Siblings with different fathers often have trouble staying intimately connected after entering adulthood, and children with an absent parent often lack the fortitude, which is mental and emotional strength, required for healthy human development.

The partner that you choose to have children with is a decision that should not be made hastily. Not everyone shows their true colors during the early stages of relationships, and a lot of people have qualities that make co-parenting a daunting challenge. For example, if you are a vegan due to your sympathy for animals, it makes little sense to have children with an avid hunter who believe that animals, due to their lesser perceived importance, should not have any rights or protections.

Although sex is natural and can be a spiritually elevating act, having sex with someone that you wish not to have children with should be avoided. I am not going to suggest that people should wait until marriage to have sex as I believe that the decision to have sex should be guided by the spirit within and not by any religious doctrine or society expectation. However, the practice of having sex with people who only turn us on physically has resulted in a lot of kids being raised in broken homes because either the mother or the father wishes not to co-parent in a united family structure with the other.

Often times, when siblings have different parents, they recognize, even if only subconsciously, that they are not the same as their siblings, which often causes some level of division. Having children that share both

mother and father unites the children together
and they are often guided by similar principles
that are taught by the same two parents who
share similar views and believe in similar
principles. If one parent teaches the children
to respect everything and everyone but the
other parent teaches the children to only be
concerned with their immediate family
members, the children will often develop a
strong case of cognitive dissonance, which
means they will have contradicting beliefs,
which then leads to mental instability and a
lack of decisiveness.

It is also widely known that children, who
are raised with one or both parents missing,
will age in years without a corresponding level
of human development. Children have
material and necessary needs from both the
mother and the father, and no child should be
disadvantaged, even if only negligently, by
being placed in a situation that doesn't
provide the various critical elements that both
parents have the power and duty to supply.
With all of this in mind, I say please be careful
when choosing intimate partners as a mistake
in choice, combined with a failure of
protection, can bring forth a disadvantaged
child. Please choose your intimate partners
carefully and be sure to consider much more

than just the way that they make you feel physically.

#4 Showing interest in the interests of others is a great way to start conversations and develop lasting relationships.

One of the most important books that aided in my development socially is *How to Win Friends and Influence People* by Dale Carnegie. One of the most valuable principles discussed in the book was the importance of showing interest in the interests in others. Basic observation often permits one to start a conversation concerning something for which the other person is engaged. Asking questions directly to others that uncover their interests and desires is a great way to get a conversation going, including with the opposite sex.

People have a tendency to appreciate people who appreciate them. Likewise, people also often gain interest in people who show interest in them. Inquiring about the interests of others also creates opportunities to develop your way of thinking, learn new things, and explore different cultures without traveling to the other person's natural environment. Most people love to talk about their interests and will do so willingly if you give them an opportunity.

Please keep in mind that each individual has his or her own challenges in life and some days may not be as well suited for conversation as others. Therefore, please do not be discouraged from approaching people who you are genuinely interested to learn more about just because you get shut down once or twice. Also, keep in mind that your energy may not be compatible with the person that you are approaching and some people that fall into this category may not be open to sharing their interests with you. If your intuition tells you to not approach a person, it is wise to follow that instruction. However, over time, if you set good intentions, you will eventually attract your tribe and your energy and gifts will likely complement their energy and gifts.

#5 Judging others isn't the job of other human beings since, for one, no one has completely clean hands, and, for two, no one except for the Most High has all of the relevant facts.

Although we all, I believe, make judgments of others, I believe that it is a habit that we as a collective should seek to avoid. For starters, no one has what I would consider to be completely clean hands. This means that to judge someone harshly for their imperfections is to treat your own imperfections as if they don't exist.

It is important to note that we all must make wise decisions when choosing who to associate with or with whom we conduct business. I am not advocating for the exclusion of discernment. A lack of discernment, when choosing friends or business associates, can have debilitating consequences. However, the problem is that we usually have harsh opinions of others, that we may even share publicly, without knowing the events that may have caused such troubling behavior. For example, a man may have been abandoned by one or both parents as a young child, which may lead to events that then lead to various personality, mental, or emotional disorders, which then lead to a large host of unfavorable actions. Not every human develops at the same rate, and some people are growing through what can be described as baptism by fire. Many people are roses that grew from the concrete, and instead of judging them for their thorns, they should be appreciated and loved, which often aids in the evolution of said person. Judging should be left to the Most High, and I think we should ask for forgiveness every time we catch ourselves being overly judgmental of others.

#6 Learning and using proper spelling and grammar is necessary, and time should be allocated to mastering the art of writing, regardless of purpose.

A person with knowledge of proper spelling, grammar, and punctuation has the power to express himself more fully when writing. This is important because so many of our communications are done electronically by email. An email or letter with poor spelling, grammar, or punctuation often leads to a bad impression of the writer, assuming the reader has sound writing skills, and can make a difference when attempting to create a new relationship or solicit investment capital for your new business.

For those who desire to write for a living, the difference between a good book and a great book, or a good article and a great article, is often the consistency and accuracy of the spelling, grammar, and punctuation. The most impactful book that helped me to improve my grammar and punctuation as a young adult was *Painless Grammar* by Rebecca

Elliott, Ph.D. The book is very easy to read and is an exceptional tool that gives a lot more in use value than what it costs to purchase.

#7 You are responsible for mastering your own energy and ensuring that you forgive everyone for whom you hold negative sentiments.

The energy that we put into the universe affects the whole, and we all contribute to the vibrations of our homes, cities, countries, and the Earth. By energy, I mean the invisible, but detectable, force that comes from our thoughts and manifest itself into feelings, intentions, and deeds. When someone commits an act that is unaligned with his or her highest self, it is highly probable that the person engaged in negative thinking and empowered his or her negative thoughts to create negative feelings that led to low vibrational intentions and actions.

It is important that we monitor our thoughts and not be consumed and controlled by them. The mind has been conditioned by the various energetic forces of the world, including television and radio, and will destroy you from within if not controlled. Although you have the right to walk around angry, harboring negative emotions, always remember that you are always responsible for your energy and that the wrong vibrations often manifest in less-than-desirable ways, resulting in some form of detriment to your own life.

Even when you think that you are justified in harboring your negative sentiments, anger and other low vibrational emotions cause damage to many of your vital organs, which is counterintuitive and self-destructive. There's a saying that the snake bite never kills anyone. It's the venom inside of the victim that actually kills the person. Be careful not to allow someone's venom to remain in you and permeate throughout your being. Meditation, protecting your karma, and the study of emotional intelligence will better prepare you to overcome negative thinking before it is allowed to manifest into your destruction. A valuable resource is *Emotional Intelligence* by Daniel Goleman.

#8 *Always do your best.*

Whether you are working on a project at your job, completing a school assignment, brushing your teeth, exercising, or making love, always do your best. This is easier said than done. I'm aware that sometimes we are tired and at less than our best, but in that moment do the absolutely best that you can. When a person fails to do the best that he or she can in any area of life, the subconscious mind is programmed to believe that the person is mediocre and mediocre effort often results in a mediocre life.

Always do the best that you can. Doing the best that you can will help you to live a life with minimal regrets. If you give your all, it is easier to live with the outcome, good or bad. However, if you know for a fact that you failed to give your best effort, resentment of self is likely to develop when things don't work out for you as desired.

ABOUT THE AUTHOR

LaFoy Orlando Thomas III, Esq. is an African-American attorney, life coach, entrepreneur, and investor. He earned his law degree from the University of Arkansas School of Law in Fayetteville, Arkansas. LaFoy has previously been licensed as a financial advisor, and his experience also includes management, mortgage lending, and real estate investing. He has been featured by various media outlets, including Business Insider. LaFoy is also an avid vegan and is the founder of the Trap Vegan clothing brand.

LaFoy is determined to share his wealth of both financial and, more importantly, spiritual wisdom with the masses and contribute to eradicating both financial and spiritual illiteracy. The author's mission is to empower the masses by making them aware of their power and responsibility as alchemists and co-creators.

Although the author believes that an innerstanding of the spiritual principles that constitute reality can begin to heal communities, he is also aware that many people who are without financial security often lack the capacity or desire to have faith in the spiritual. This dynamic often creates an environment where moral compasses are suppressed and principles, or codes of ethics, are suspended.

The author believes that his approach to healing communities and families by integrating financial and spiritual concerns is the wave of the future. He believes that more private teachers and coaches will soon recognize the downside of addressing the spiritual without addressing the financial and of improving the financial without considering the impact of spiritual principles on the lives of clients. To book a life-coaching session or a paid speaking engagement with LaFoy, please visit GWLifeCoaching.com. For a signed copy of any of his books, please visit GWSigned.com.

Made in the USA
Columbia, SC
20 December 2019